COLORS OF NEW ENGLAND

Eduardo Brazao

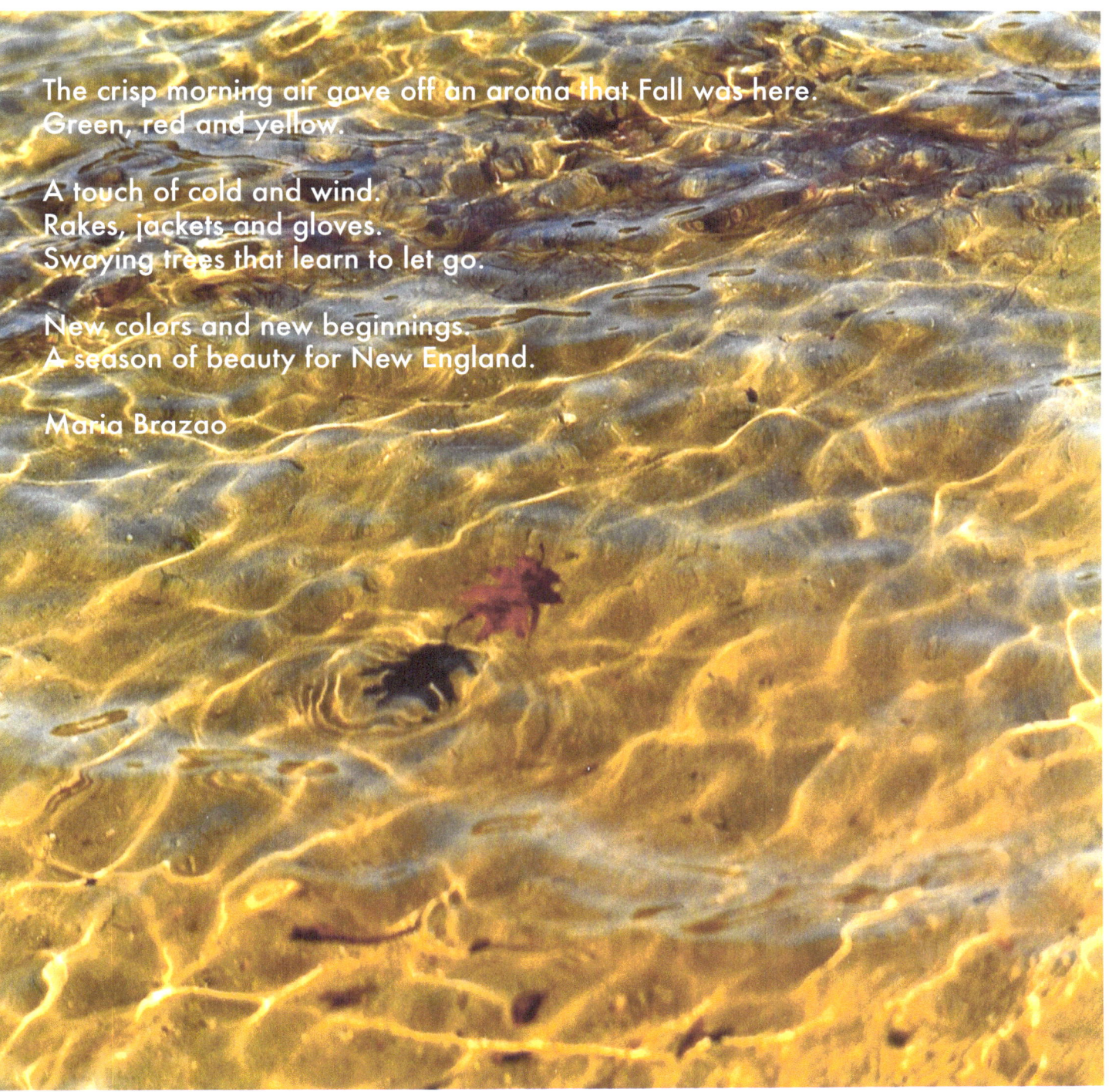

The crisp morning air gave off an aroma that Fall was here.
Green, red and yellow.

A touch of cold and wind.
Rakes, jackets and gloves.
Swaying trees that learn to let go.

New colors and new beginnings.
A season of beauty for New England.

Maria Brazao

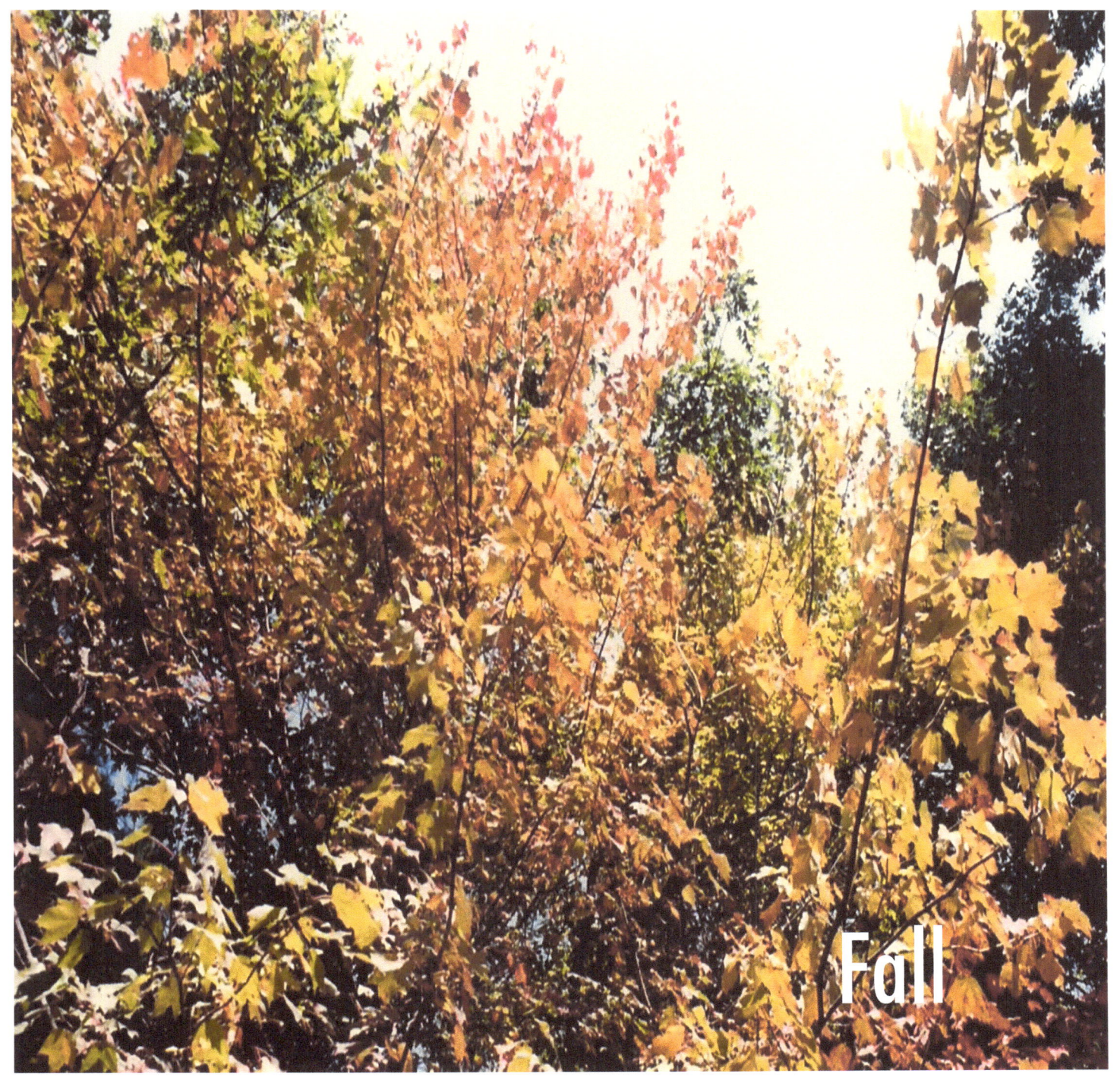

Fall

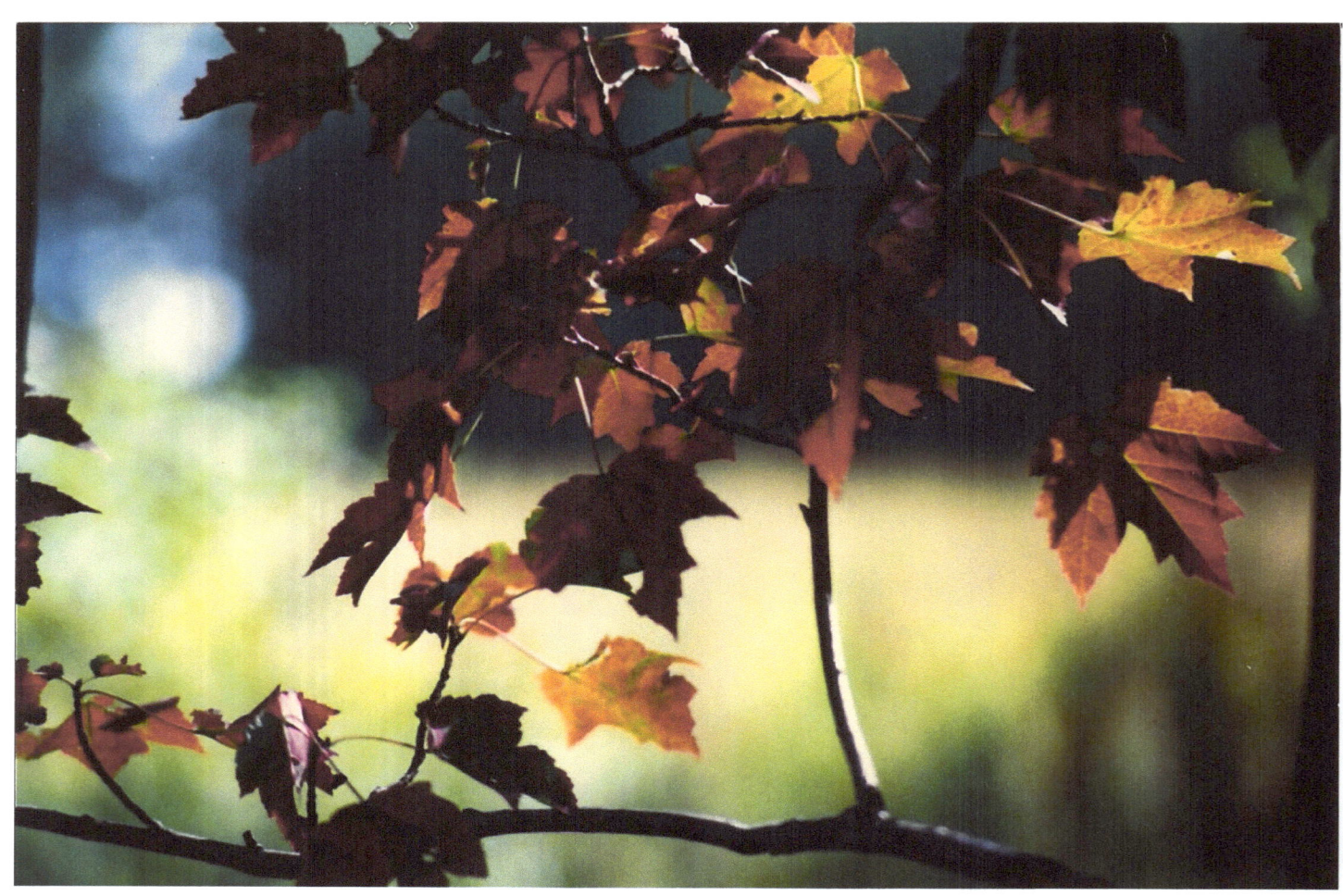

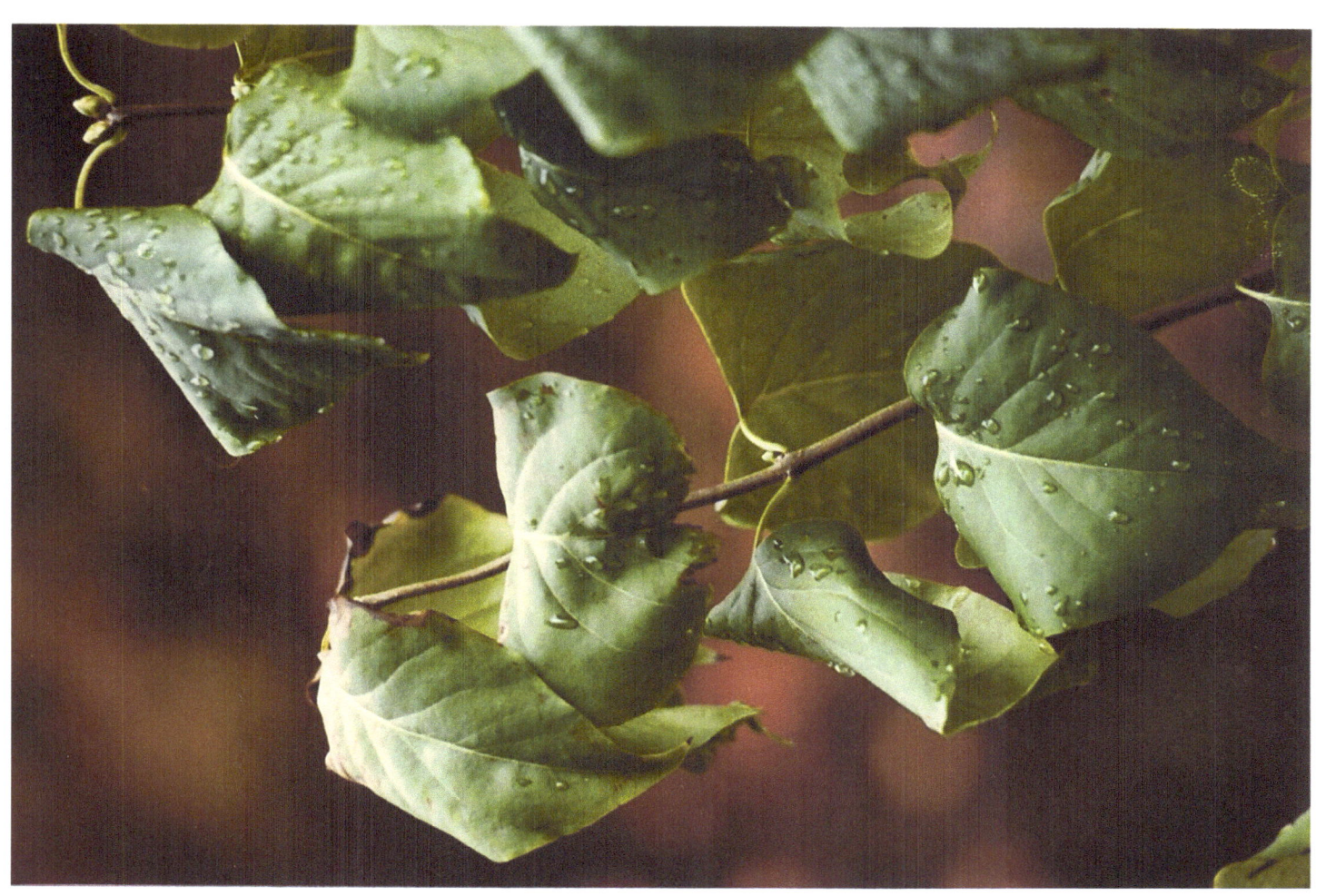

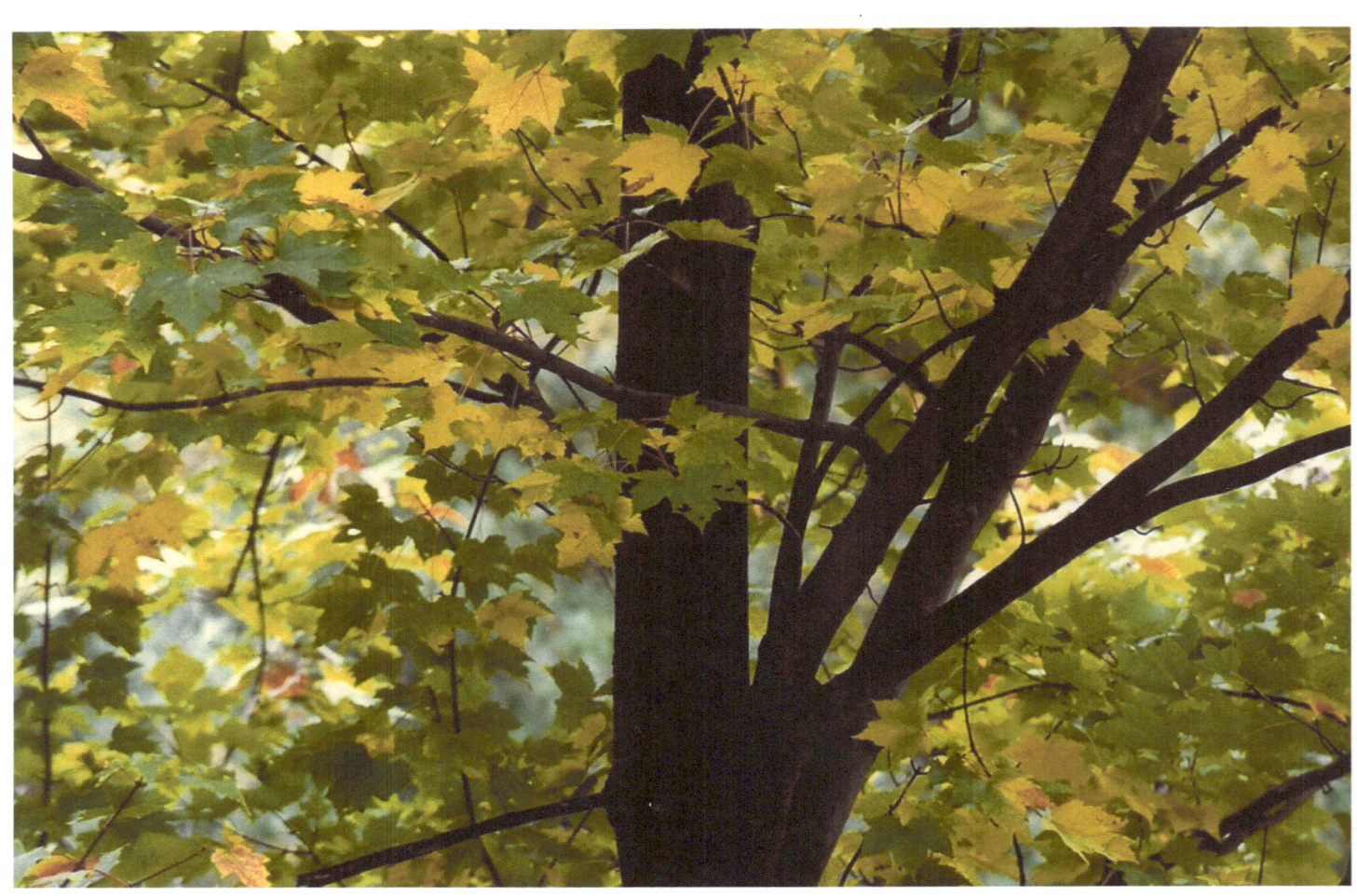

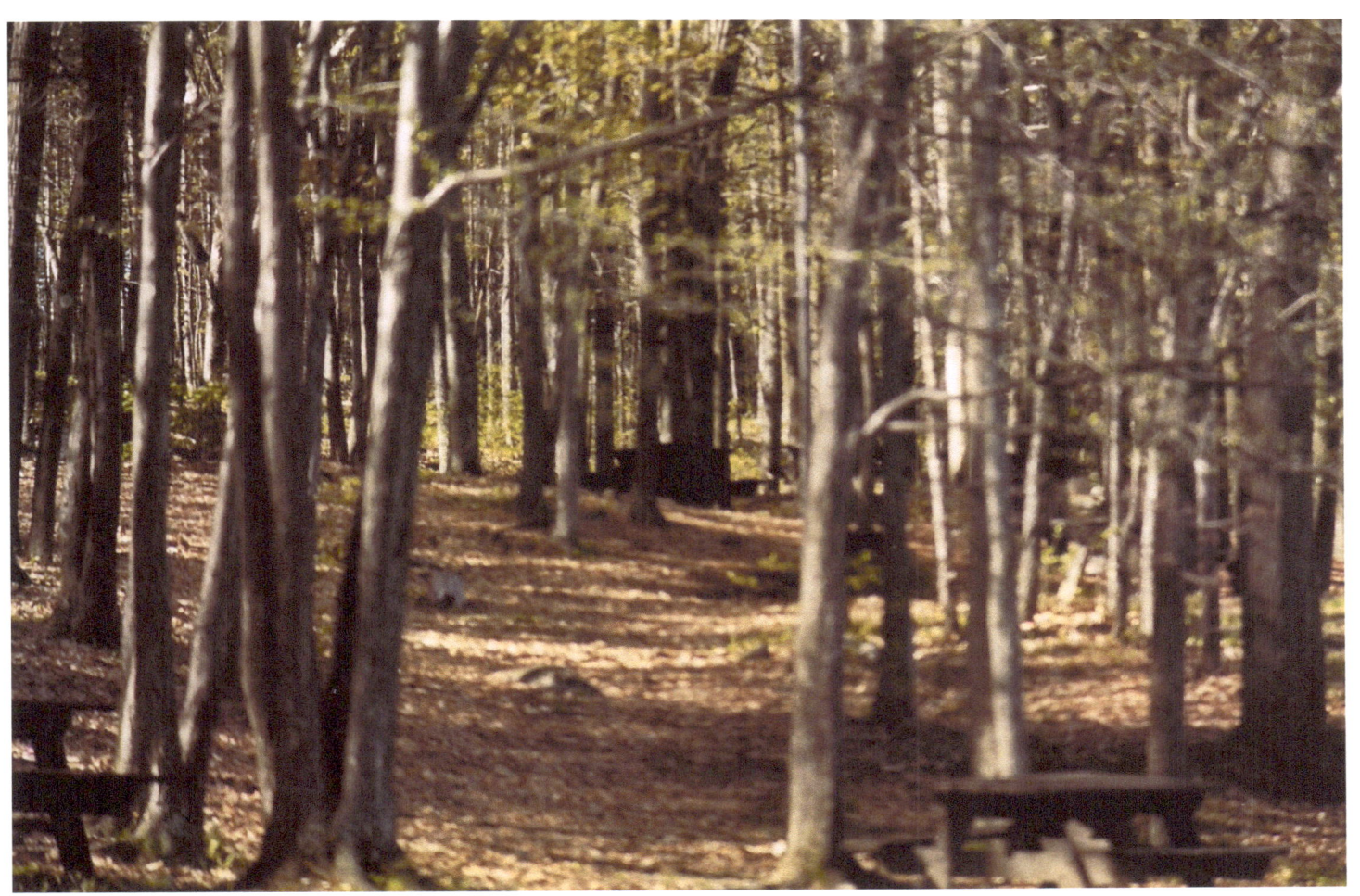

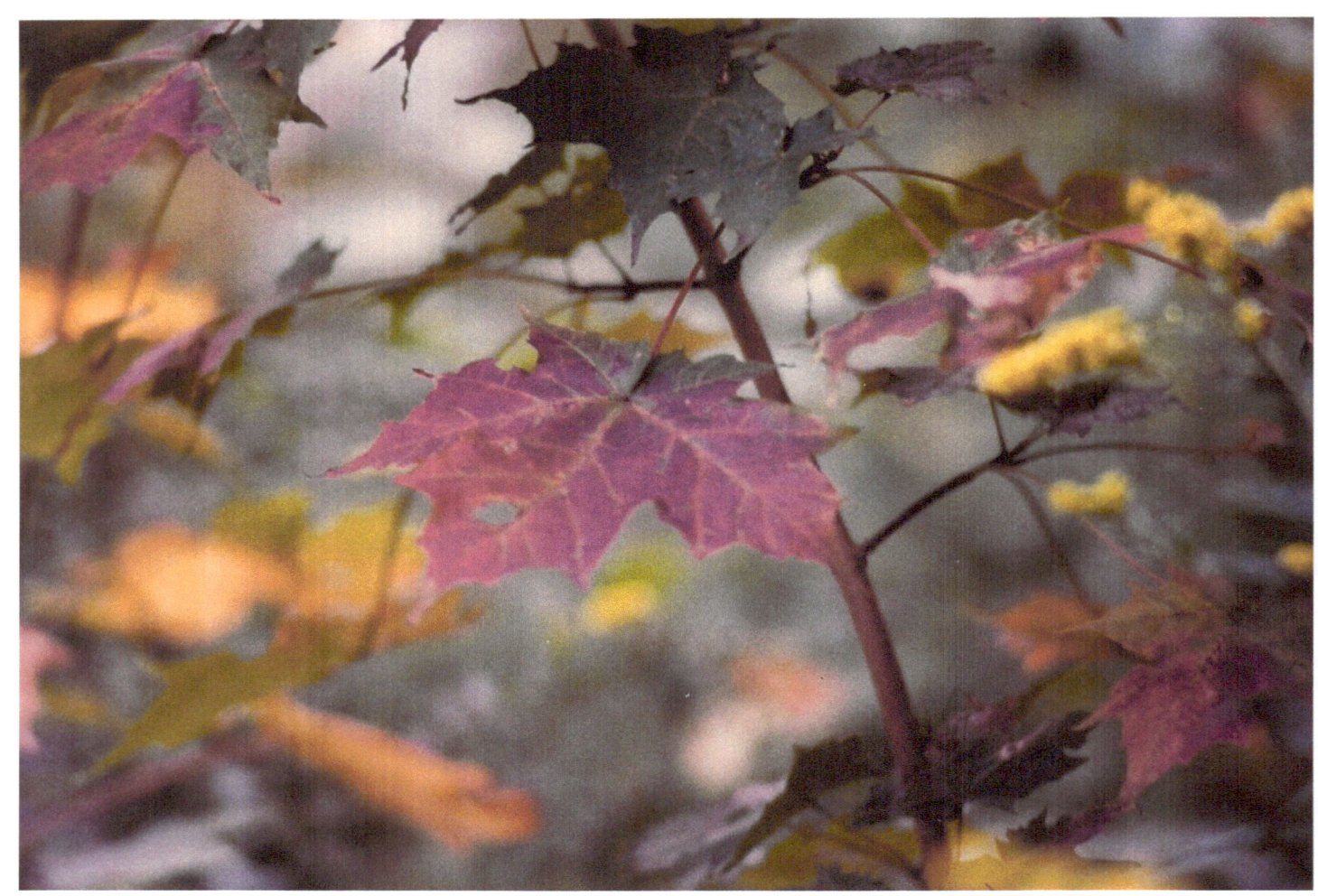

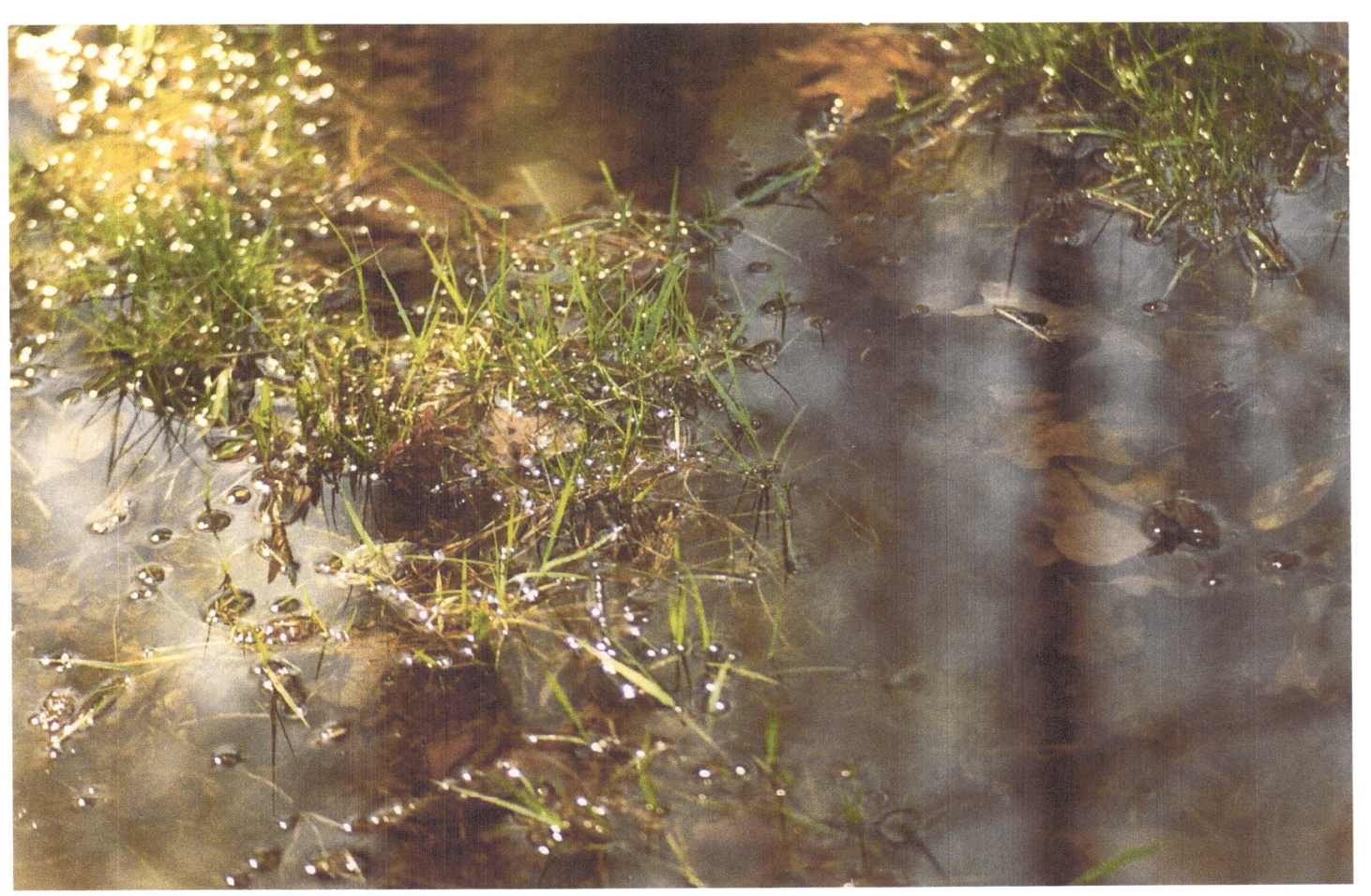

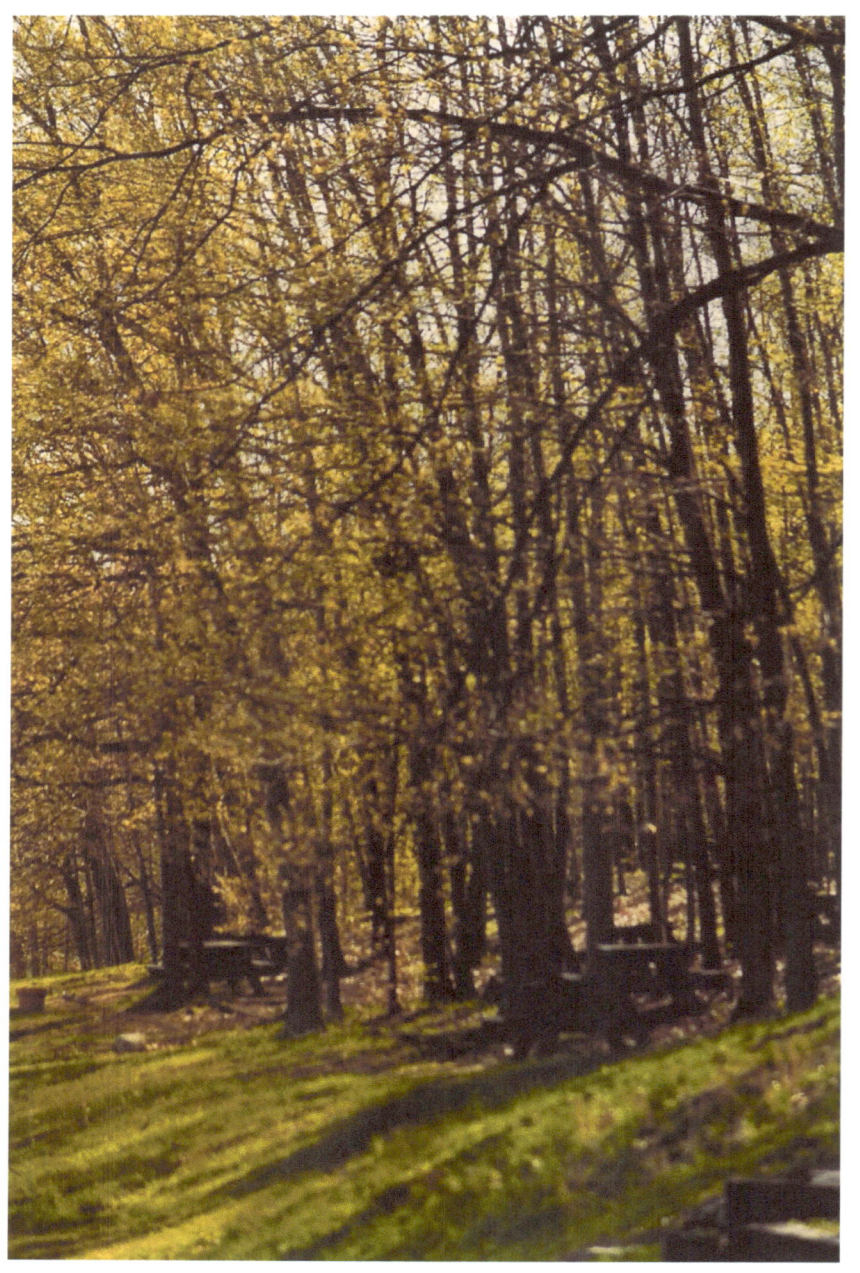

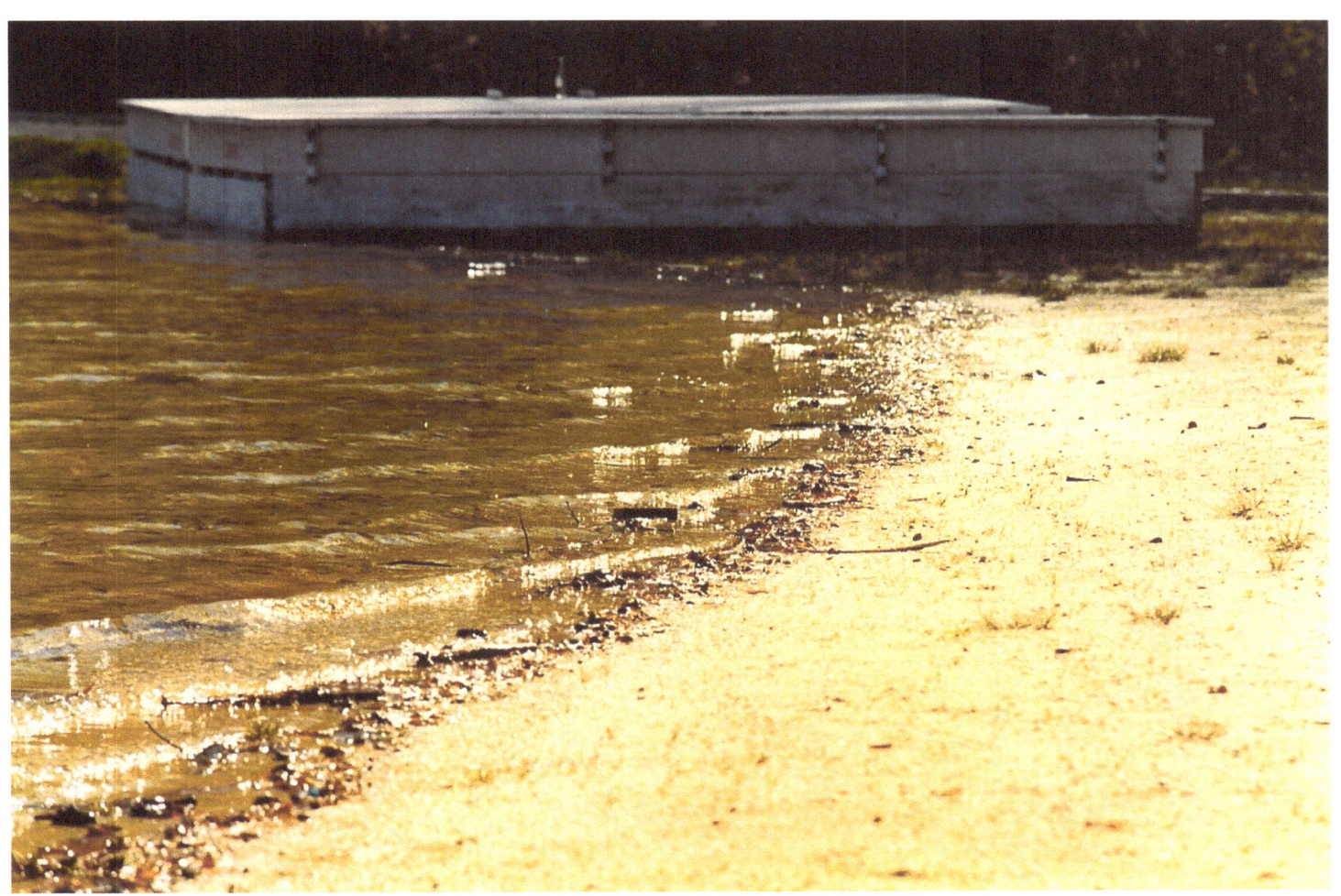

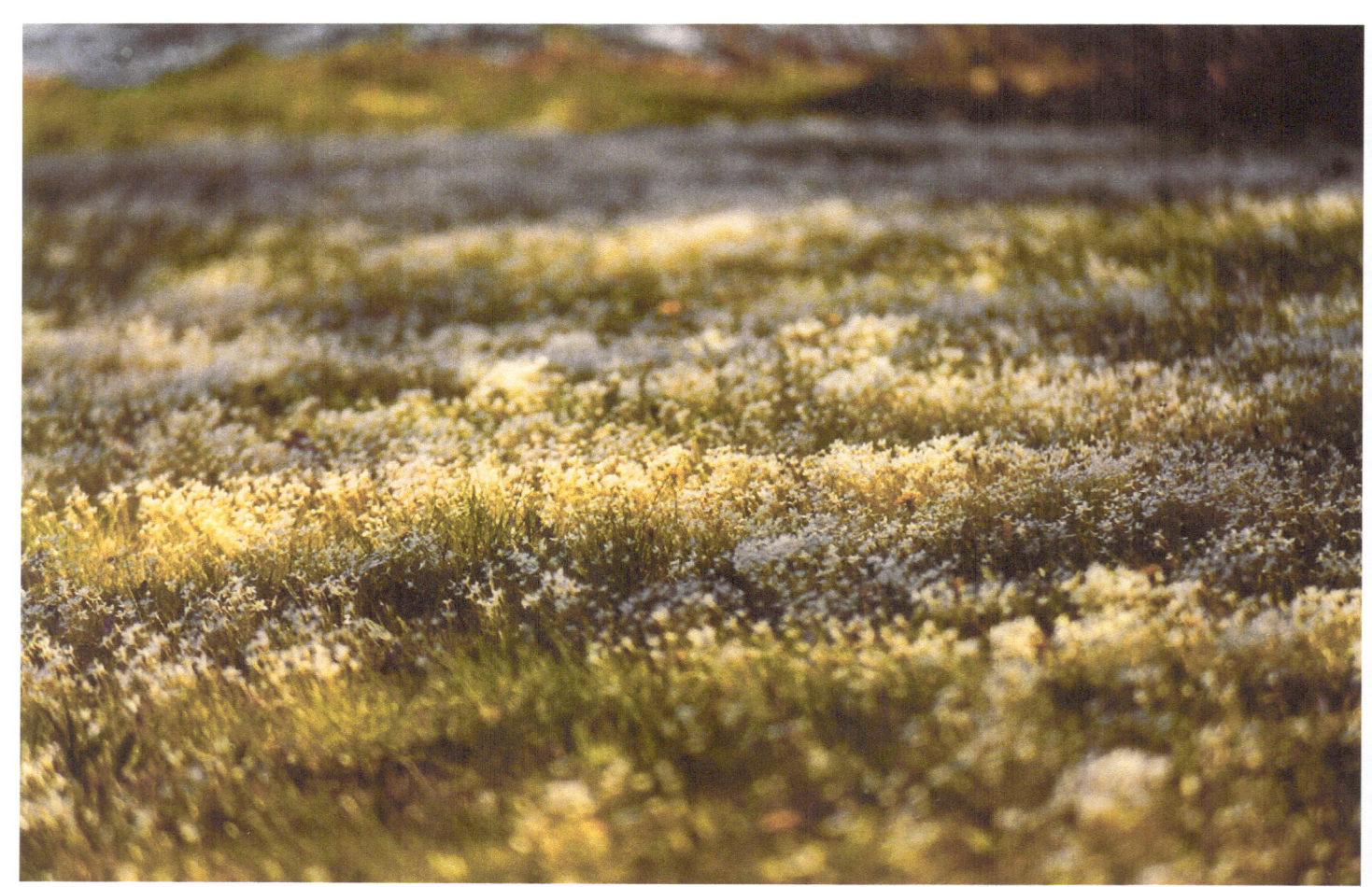

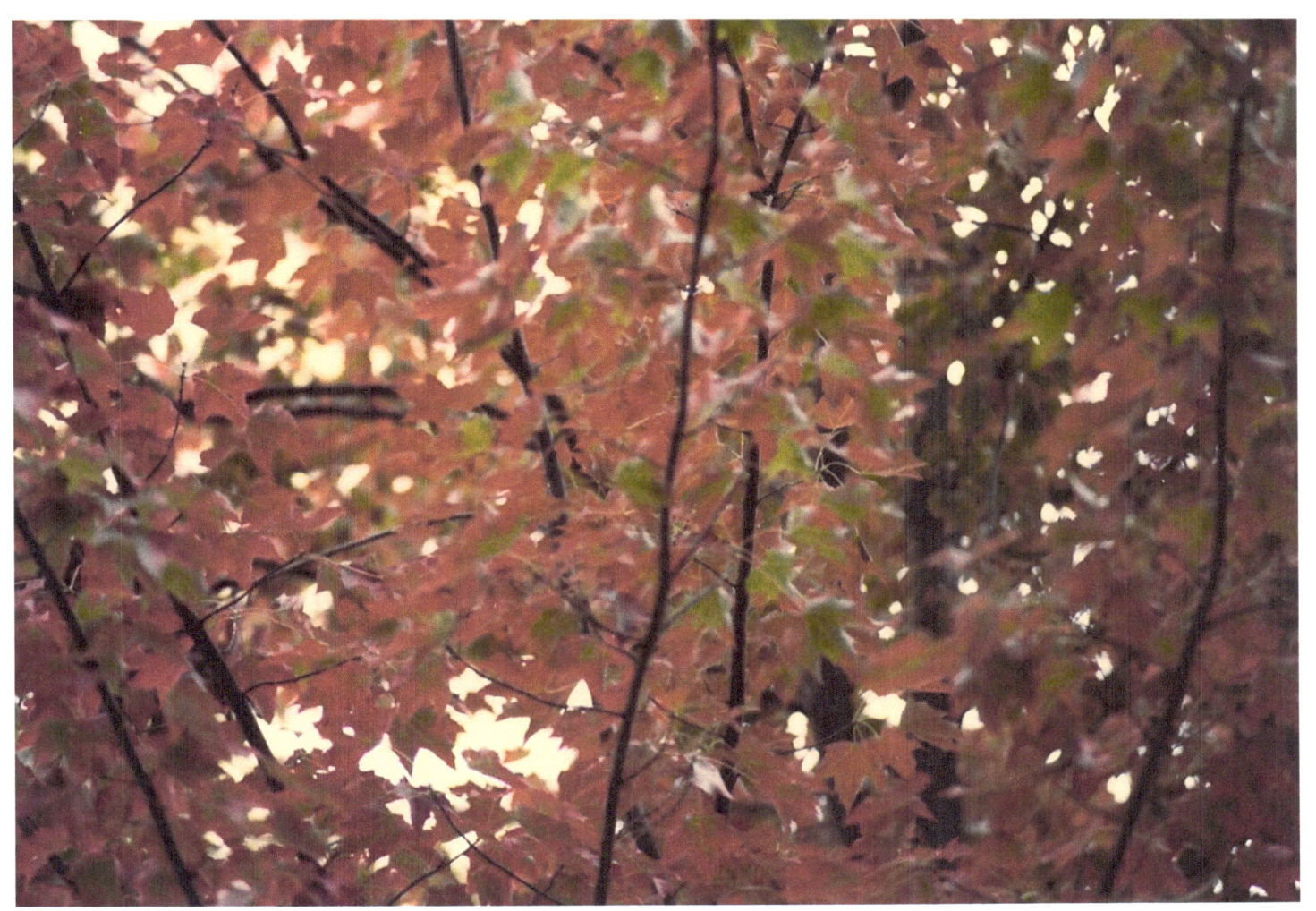

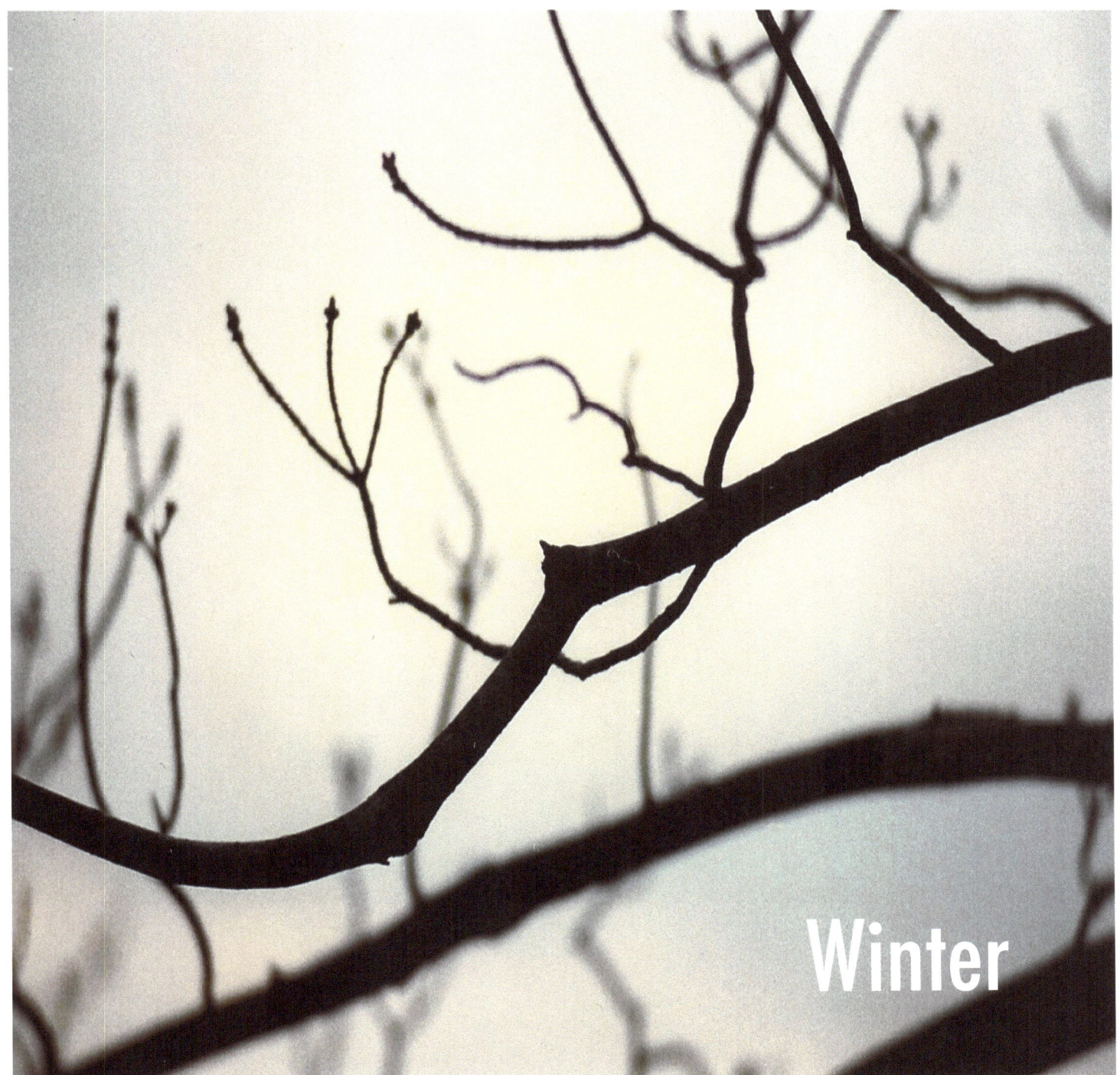

Winter

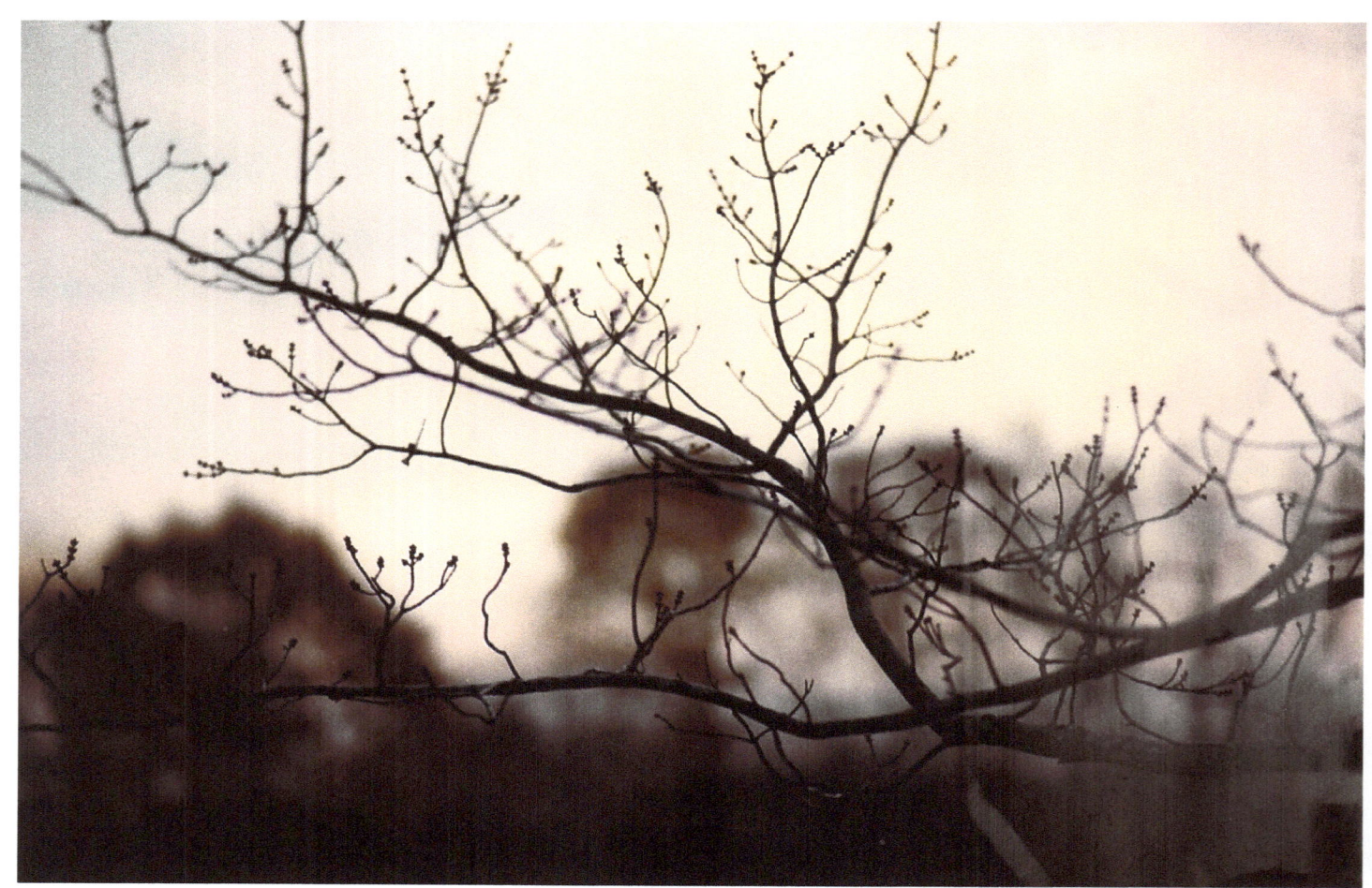

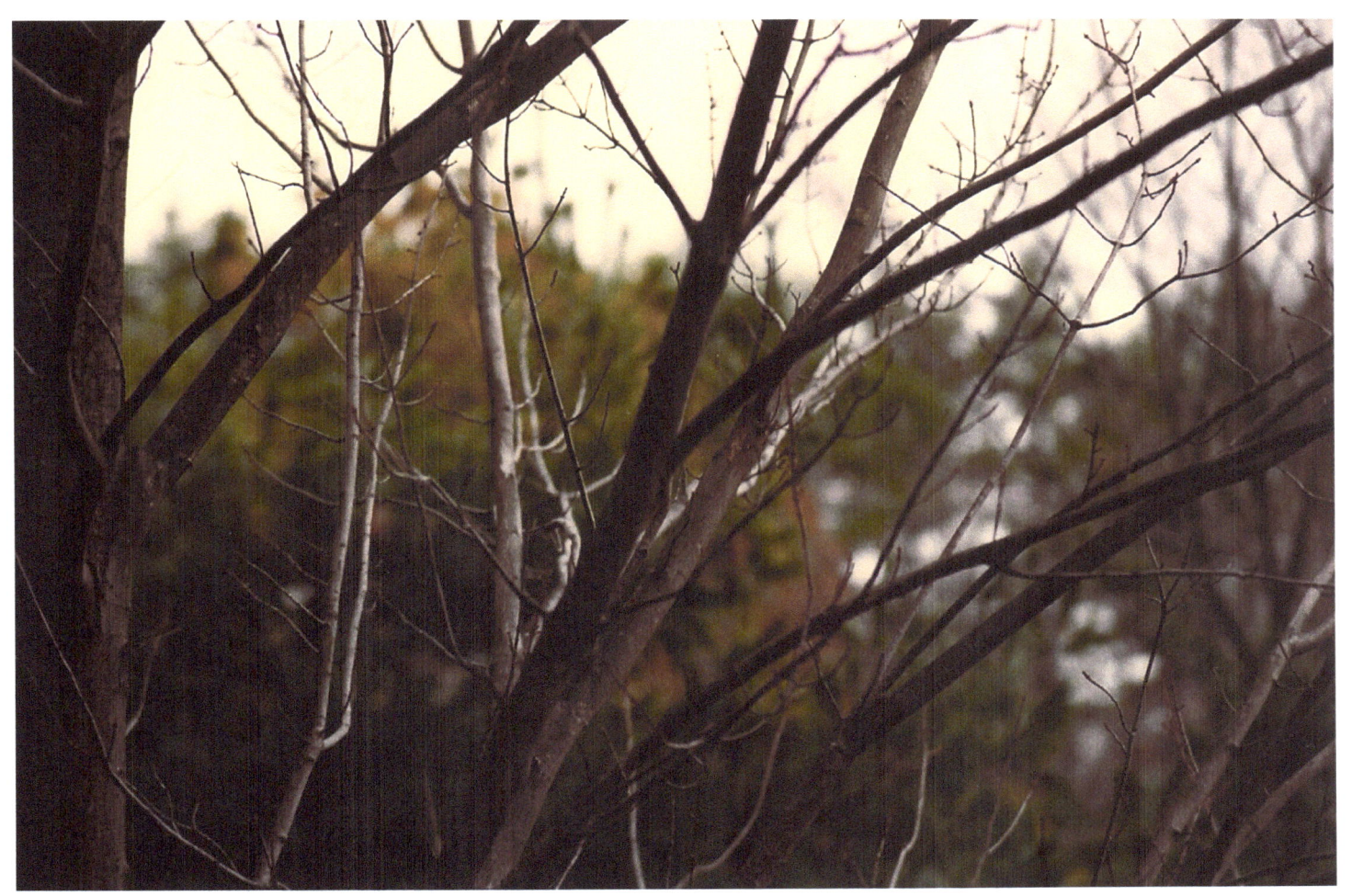

19

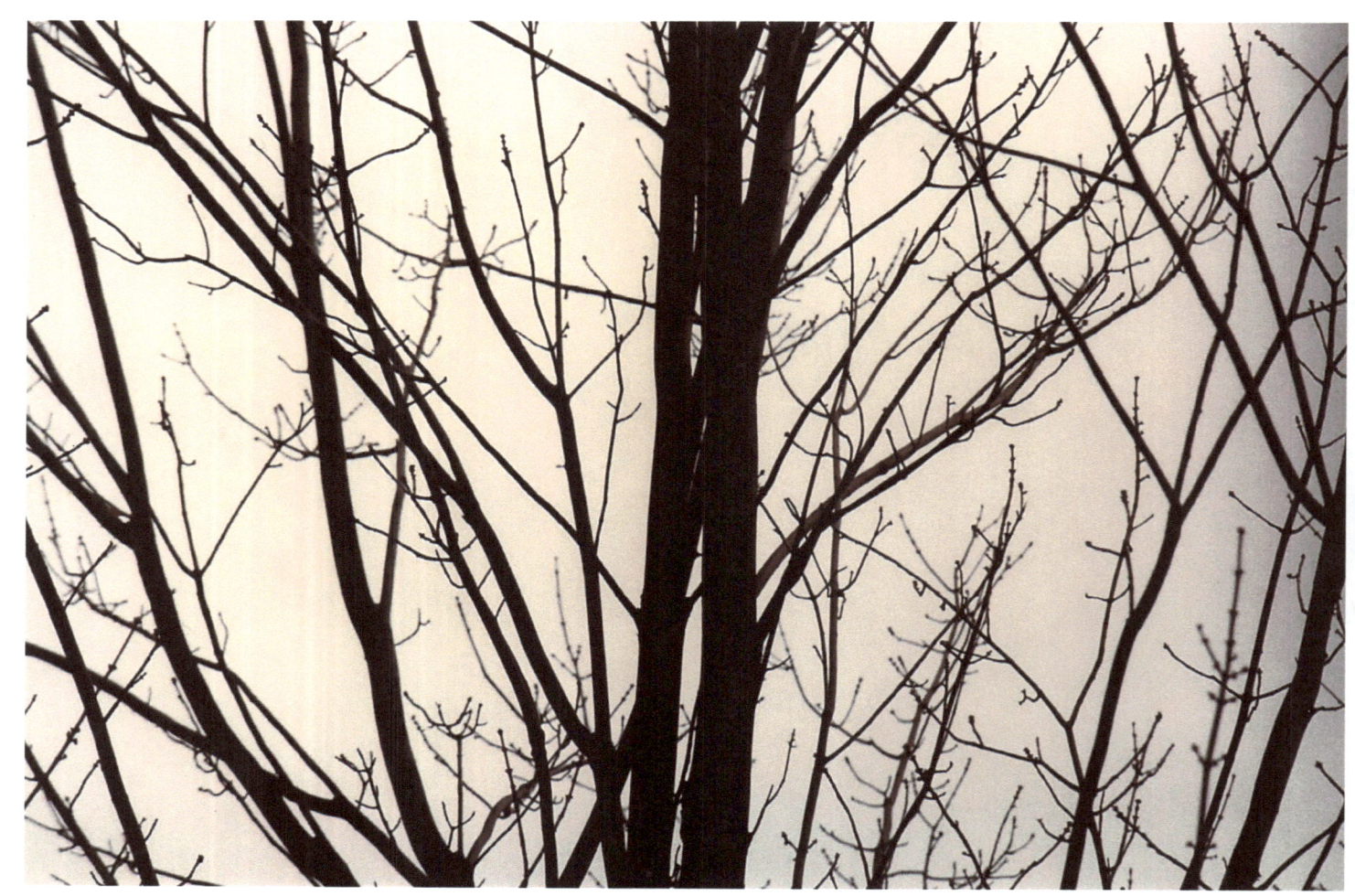

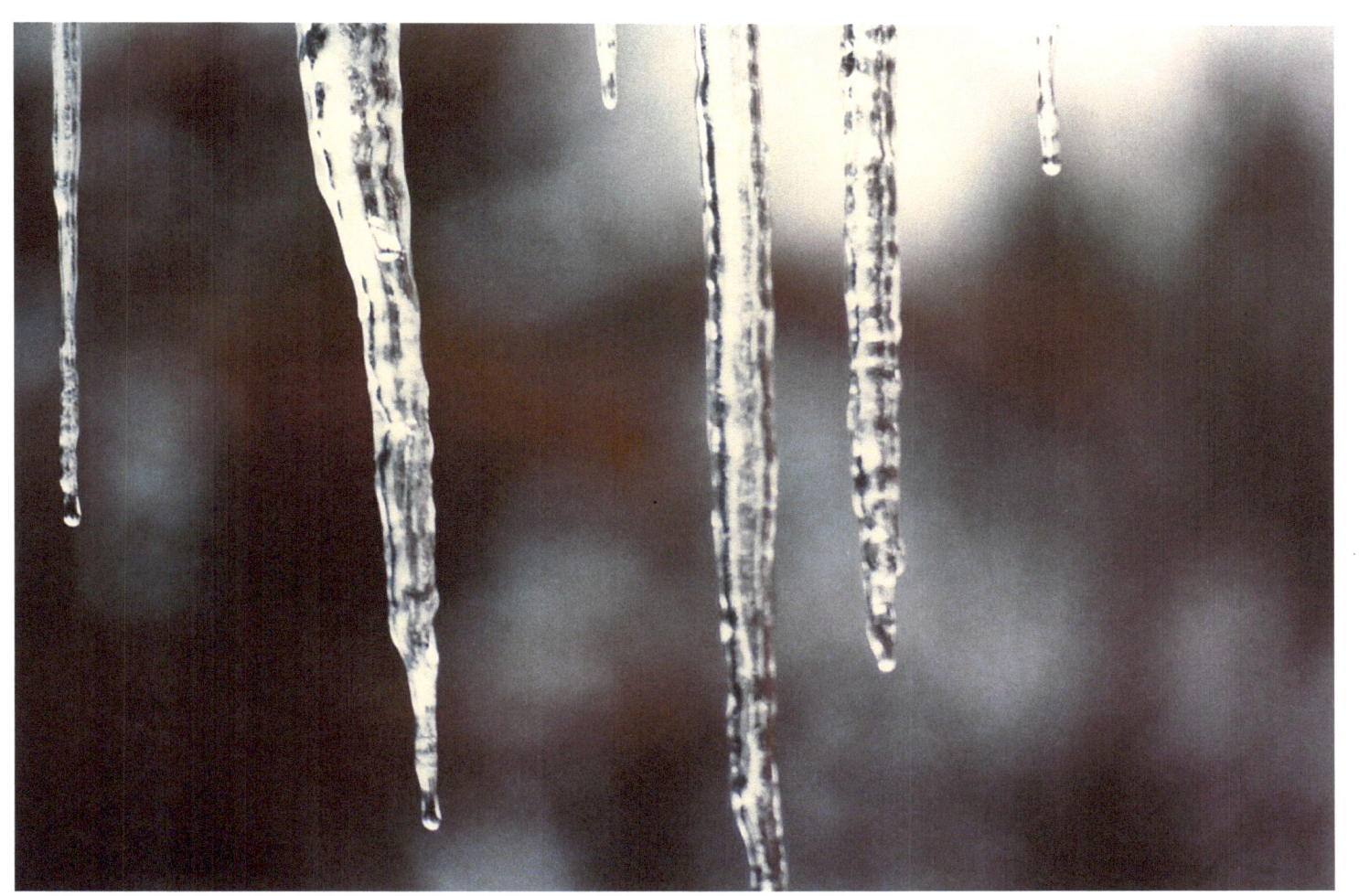

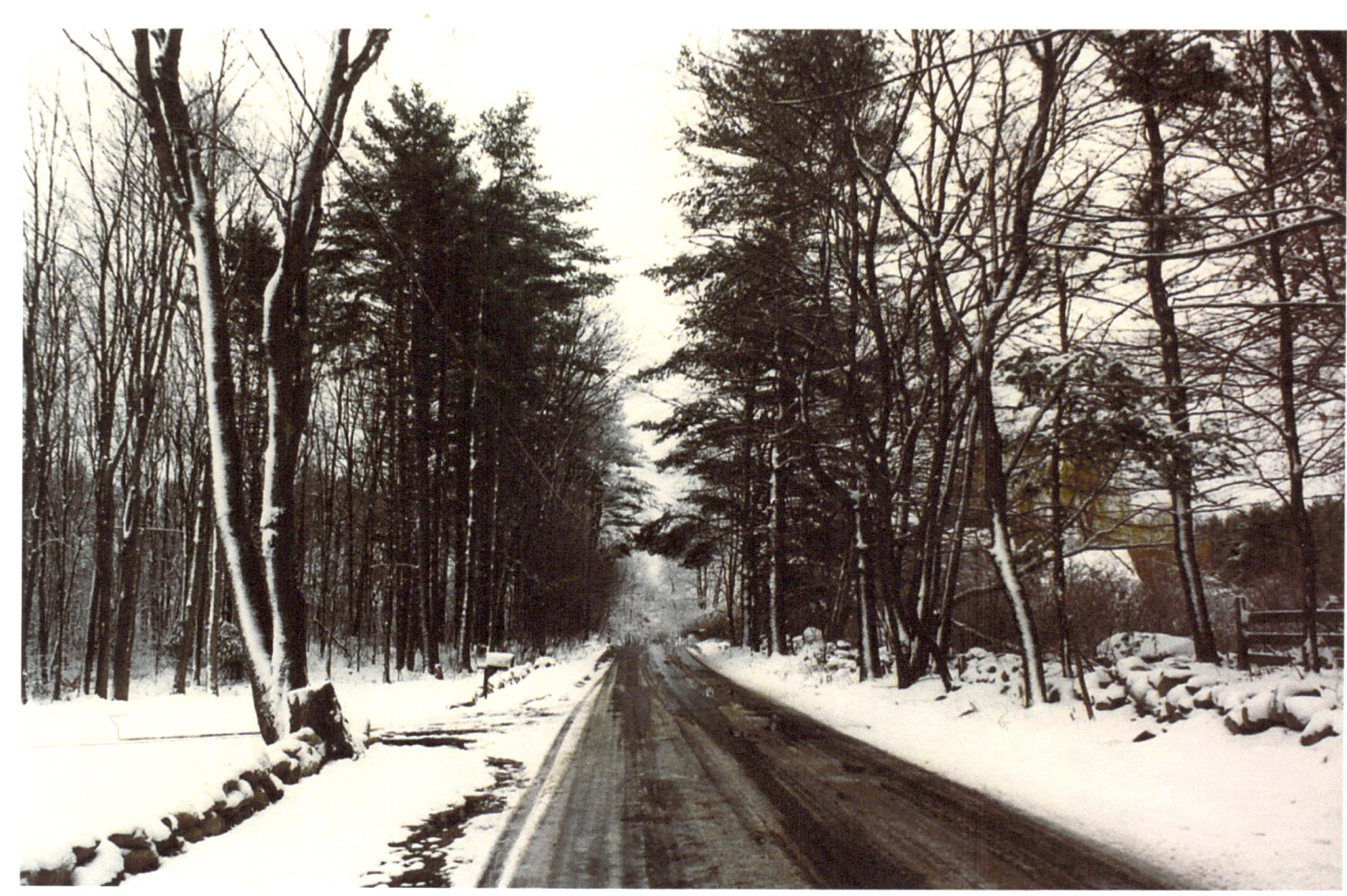

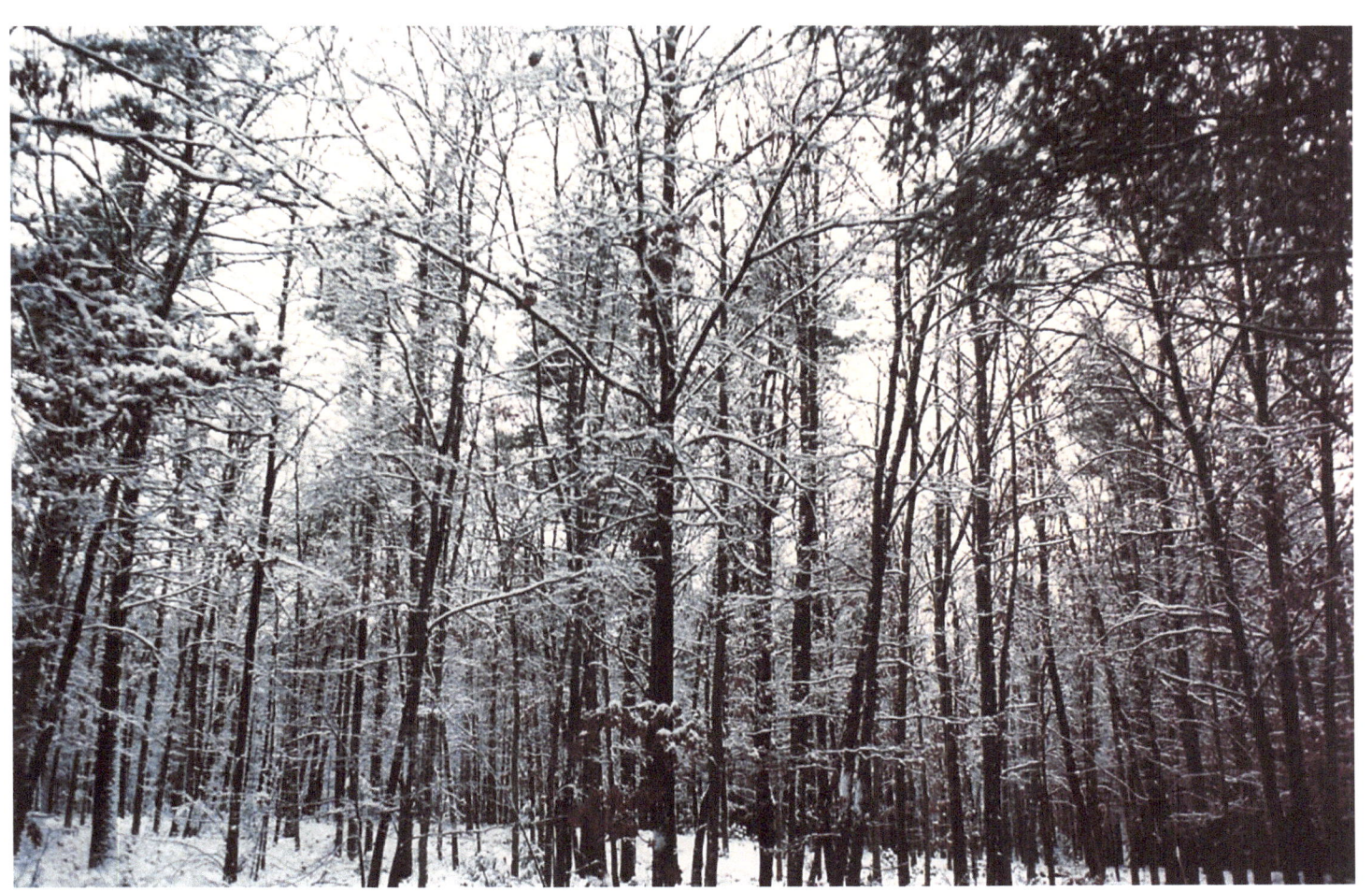

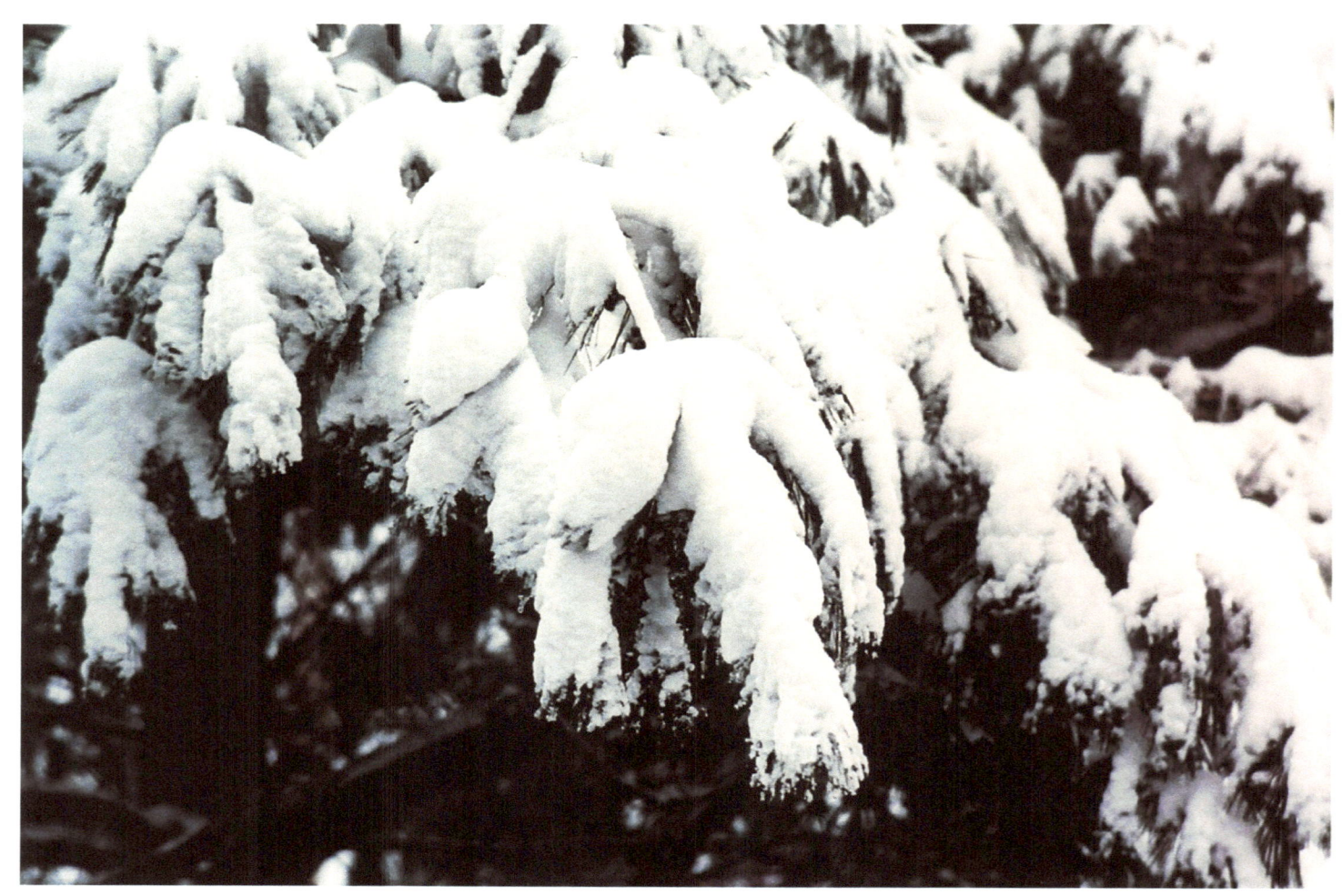

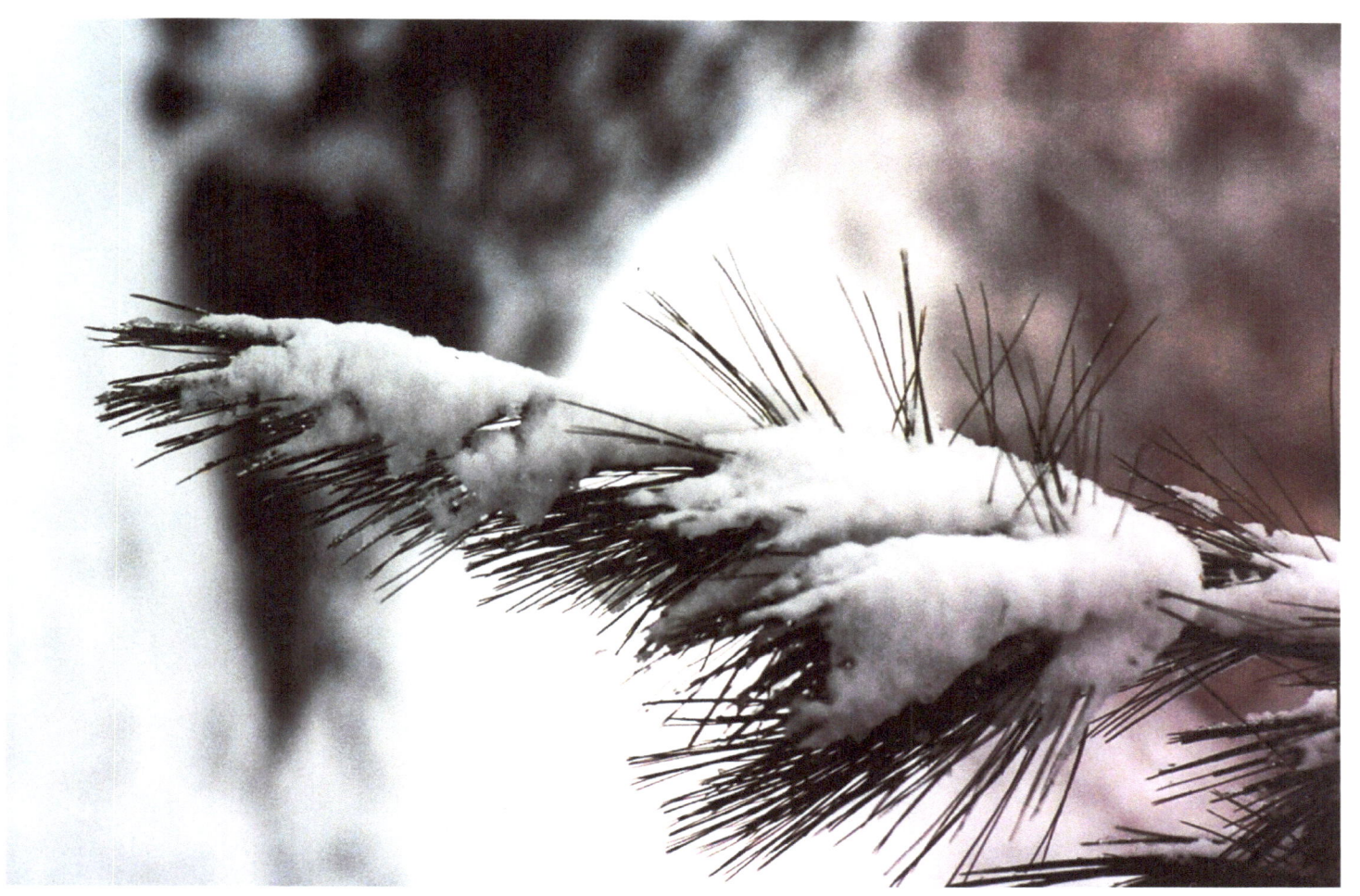

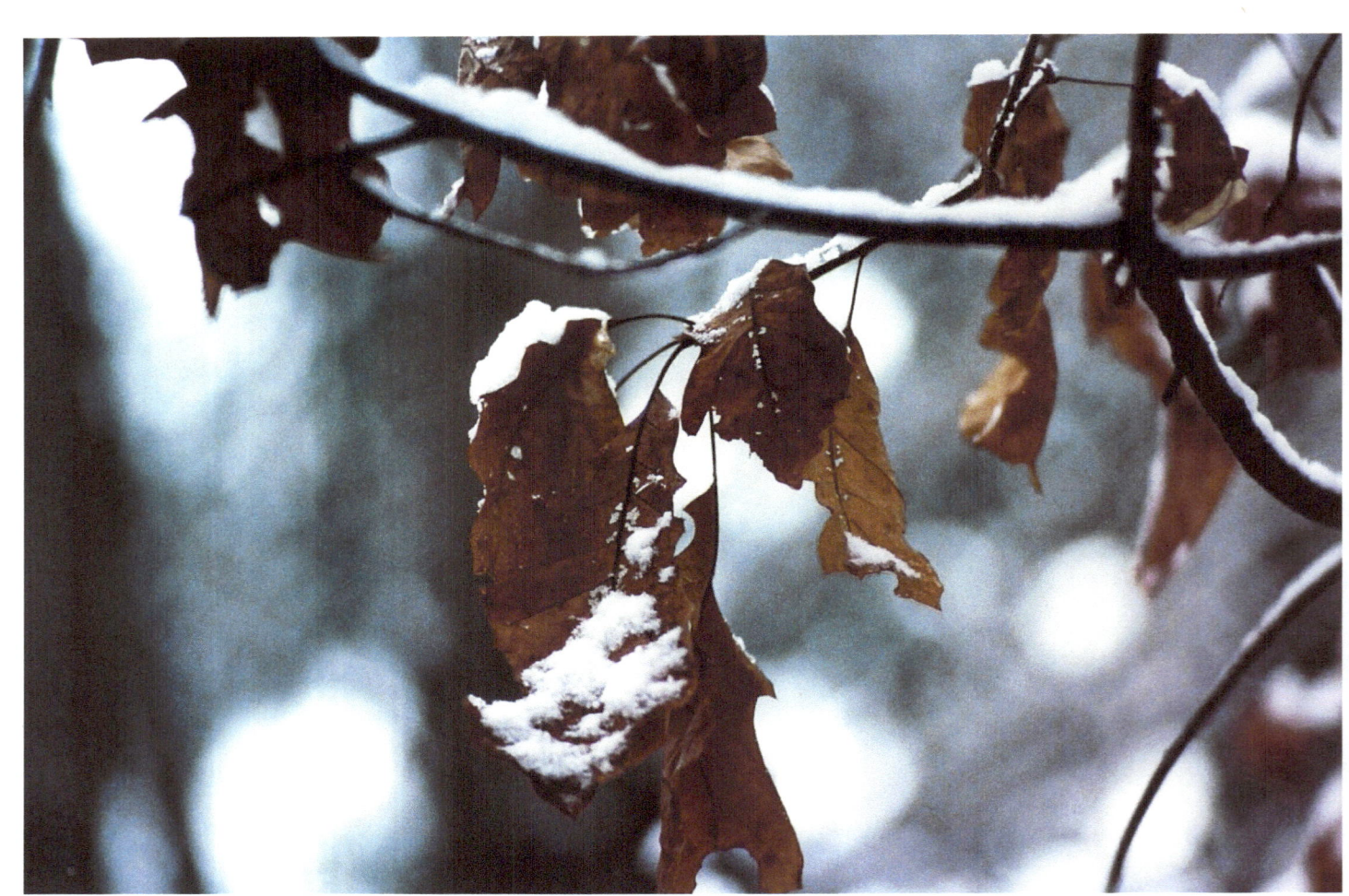

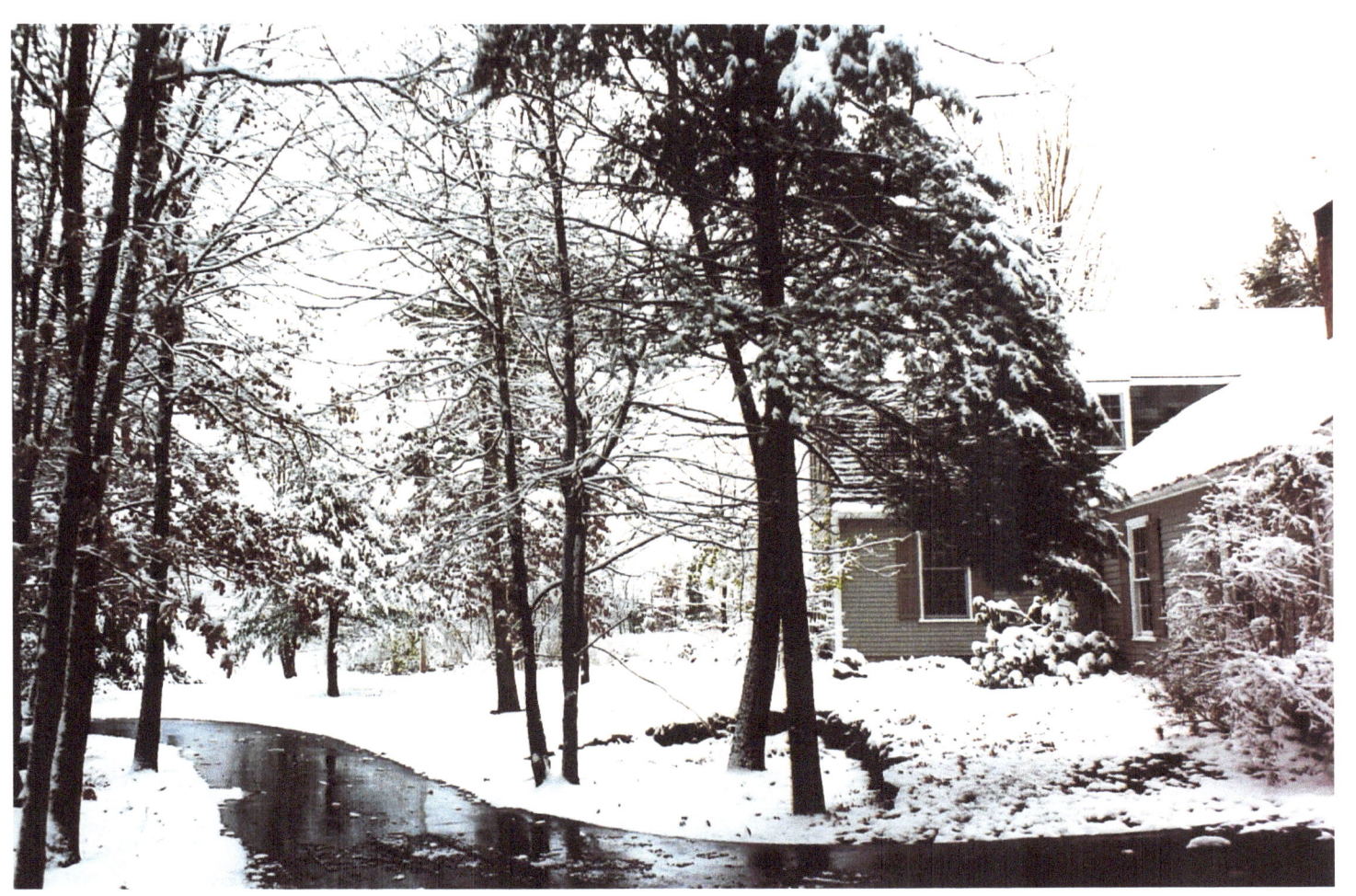

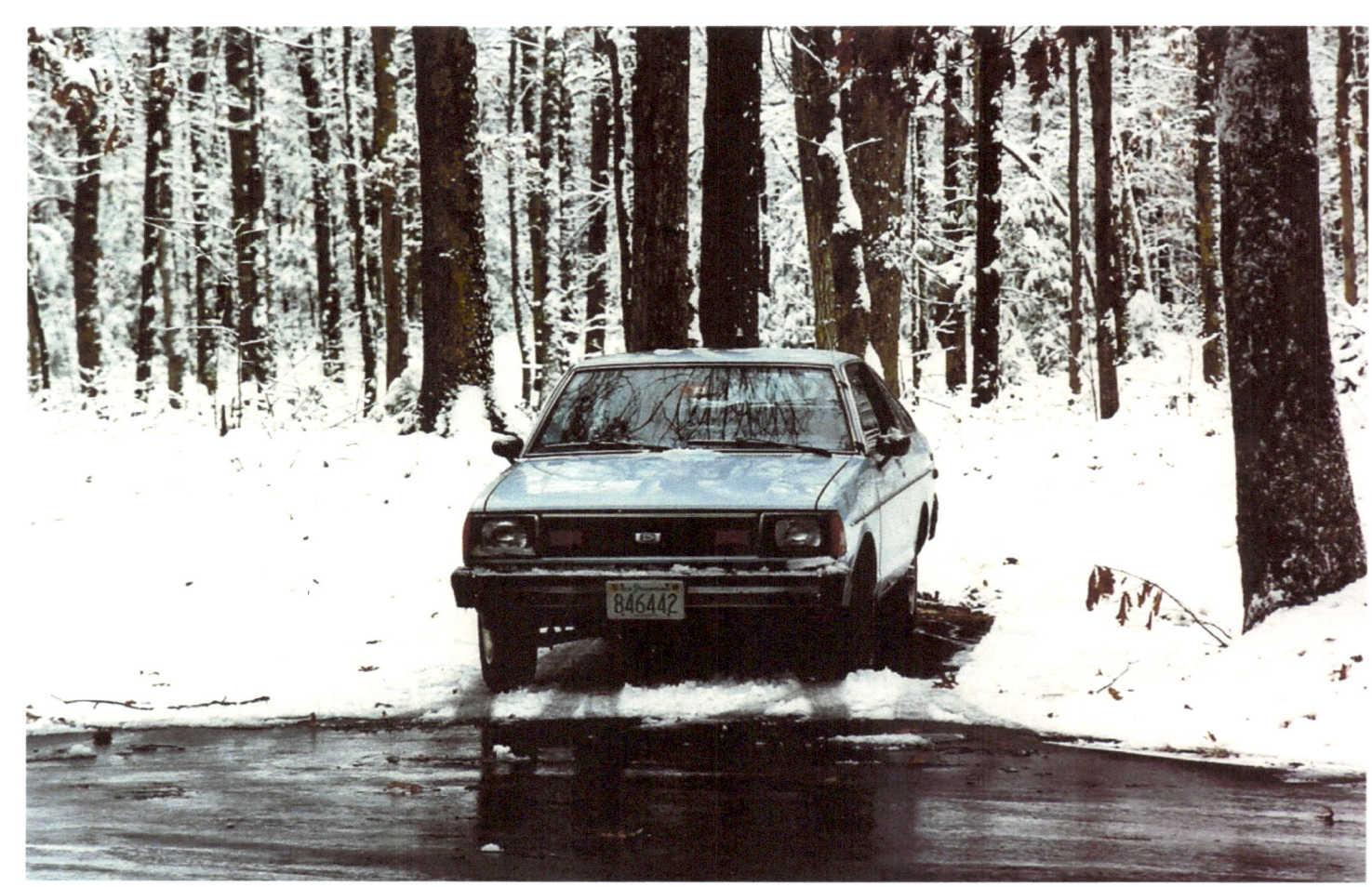

About the Author

Eduardo Brazao was born in Lisbon, Portugal. His family moved to Rio de Janeiro, Brazil, when he was nine years old. He spent his youth living across from Baia de Guanabara, facing Sugar Loaf Mountain and enjoying the beautiful cidade maravilhosa. He returned to Lisbon at the age of 16, where he finished high school and three years of law school. He moved to the United States in 1987, and graduated with a degree in Business Administration from Rivier University of New Hampshire. In 1990 he moved back to Lisbon where he worked for the Portuguese government for seven years and completed his MBA in International Management. A Business Development career opportunity to work in the Latin America markets took him back to New Hampshire in 1997. Three years later, he was transferred to Dallas, Texas, and he ultimately settled in Virginia in 2004. In spite of his full-time in the telecommunications industry and his love for technology, photography has always been a passion.

www.ingramcontent.com/pod-product-compliance
Lightning Source LLC
Chambersburg PA
CBHW050423180526
45159CB00005B/2391